SMART BEHAVIOUR

INSTALLATION

GUIDE

Put Your Kid's Growth on Autopilot, Feel Proud and Make them Super Humans

SMART BEHAVIOUR INSTALLATION GUIDE

Put Your Kid's Growth on Autopilot, Feel Proud and Make them Super Humans

Khumukcham
Roshan Singh

Worldwide Published by
Pendown Press

PENDOWN PRESS LLP

An ISO 9001 & ISO 14001 Certified Co.,

Regd. Office: 3767A, Kanhaiya Nagar,

Tri Nagar, Delhi-110035

Ph.: 8130886000, 9650072927

E-mail: info@pendownpress.com

Branch Office: 1A/2A, 20, Hari Sadan, Ansari Road,

Daryaganj, New Delhi-110002

Ph.: 011-45794768

Website: PendownPress.com

Edition: 2025

ISBN: 978-93-6338-525-2

Layout and Cover Designed by Pendown Graphics Team
Printed and Bound in India by Thomson Press India Ltd.

Table of Contents

CHAPTER - 1

WHO WANTS SMART KIDS?

So, how many of you want your children to be
super happy, successful and prosperous?

How many of you would love to have a blueprint or tool
to navigate the ups and downs of parenting smoothly and
easily?

All of you who answered a resounding yes, please read further
and the rest of you can put the book down, congratulations, you
seem to be doing a great job at raising your children!

WHAAAT? None of you is willing to put the book down!

Okay, okay, okay! I get it, raising happy and fulfilled children isn't easy and I am here to help you with raising smart & adaptive STAR KIDS.

The Parenting Code

In the ever-evolving landscape of parenthood, where the challenges and opportunities of the digital age intertwine with age-old wisdom, a new paradigm is emerging.

Welcome to this revolutionary guide that explores the concept of "Parenting by Code," a groundbreaking approach that sees parents as programmers, **shaping the behavioural code of their children for a future defined by innovation and adaptability.**

As humans, we are all creatures of programming. Our programming, of course, is influenced by various parameters such as genetics, education, culture, role modelling etc.

In this age of information and technology, **it wouldn't be wrong to say that parenting is similar to writing a complex software program,** where every line of code, every input, and every output plays a crucial role in moulding the character and potential of the next generation.

This book delves into the art and science of parenting, offering insights and strategies for parents who seek to actively influence their children's behaviours, attitudes, and ultimately, their success in a rapidly changing world.

The Code of Influence

In this book, you will explore the fundamental principles that govern the parent-child relationship and the subtle ways in which parental behaviours serve as the primary code that shapes a child's understanding of the world. Uncover the power dynamics at play and learn how to harness the potential for positive influence.

Debugging Negative Patterns

Just as in programming, bugs can disrupt the functionality of a program, negative behavioural patterns can hinder a child's development. Within the pages of this book, you will discover effective strategies for identifying and debugging these patterns, ensuring a smoother and more optimized upbringing.

The Language of Encouragement

Further, you will understand the importance of positive reinforcement and encouragement in fostering a growth mindset in your child. Learn to use the language of empowerment to build resilience and instill a passion for learning and exploration.

Building a Supportive Framework

You will also examine the role of the family environment as the programming framework for a child's development. Explore ways to create a nurturing and supportive atmosphere that promotes curiosity, creativity, and collaboration.

Upgrading Parenting Strategies for the Digital Age

In a world dominated by technology, explore how parents can navigate the challenges of screen time, social media, and digital distractions. Learn to leverage technology as a tool for learning and growth while maintaining a healthy balance.

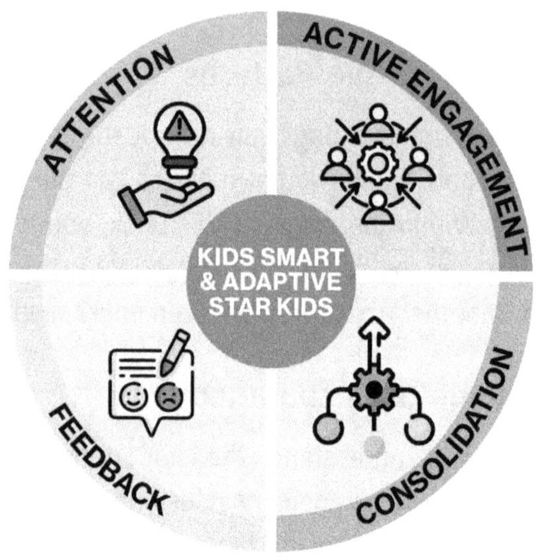

Attention, active engagement, feedback, and consolidation are the 4 pillars of learning for making KIDS SMART and ADAPTIVE STAR KIDS.

Learning is a biological adaptation, and like any other adaptation is the outcome of evolution by natural selection. A learning environment is much more than what you see visually.

As we embark on this journey of "Parenting by Code," remember that the power to shape the future lies in the hands of parents who understand the intricacies of the code they impart to their children. Join us on this transformative exploration of parenthood, where the code you write today determines the possibilities your child will unlock tomorrow.

In the following chapters, we will deep dive into understanding the classification of various generations, their mindsets, coding blueprints and how we can modify these blueprints to **achieve the goal of developing amazing star kids** who not only excel according to the needs of the times but blossom into their full potential as per their aptitudes. To top it all they are kind, compassionate and responsible citizens contributing to growth and harmony in society.

We will begin with understanding how each generation is unique and how it influences the next..

❑ ❑ ❑ ❑

CHAPTER - 2

LET'S GET GEN SAVVY!
Understanding Generations & Their Power Play

A Historical Tapestry

Let's embark on the journey of nurturing smart, star kids by first understanding how generations are categorized so that it will make it easier for you to understand the role & interplay of generations impacting the behaviour of children.

In the vast tapestry of human history, generations weave their own unique threads, each generation contributes to the evolving narrative of society.

Today, as we stand amidst the whirlwind of technological advancement and societal transformation, it is crucial to understand the intricate dynamics of the generations and how they shape our present and future.

With each passing era, the flag of power, influence, and innovation passes from one generation to the next, and each generation imprints its mark on the world stage in its unique fashion.

To begin with, let's see how the generations are categorized-

Generation Names & Timeline Classification

- The Greatest Generation – Born 1901-1924.
- The Silent Generation – Born 1925-1945.
- The Baby Boomer Generation – born 1946-1964.
- Generation X – Born 1965-1979.
- Millennials – Born 1980-1994.
- Generation Z – Born 1995-2012.
- Generation Alpha – Born 2013 – 2025.

Baby Boomers Go Boom-Boom-Boom

Running the world as we see it today are the **Baby Boomers**, a generation characterized by their resilience, determination, and sheer numbers.

Born in the aftermath of World War II, they witnessed unprecedented economic growth and societal change. Alongside them stand the champions of resilience, the **Silent Generation,** whose quiet fortitude shaped the world in the post-war era.

Yet, as time marches on, the reins of power are gradually shifting. **Generation X,** often described as the bridge between the past and the future, now holds a significant share of influence, bringing with them a blend of pragmatism and innovation.

Following closely behind are the **Millennials,** a generation marked by their technological prowess, ambition, and idealism. However, they grapple with their own set of challenges, from economic uncertainty to the ever-looming shadow of technology addiction.

Amidst this mosaic of generations, a new combo emerges – **Generation Z** and **Generation Alpha**.

Born into a world of smartphones and social media, they are the digital natives, effortlessly navigating the internet and technology.

But beyond their technological fluency lies a deeper potential waiting to be unlocked.

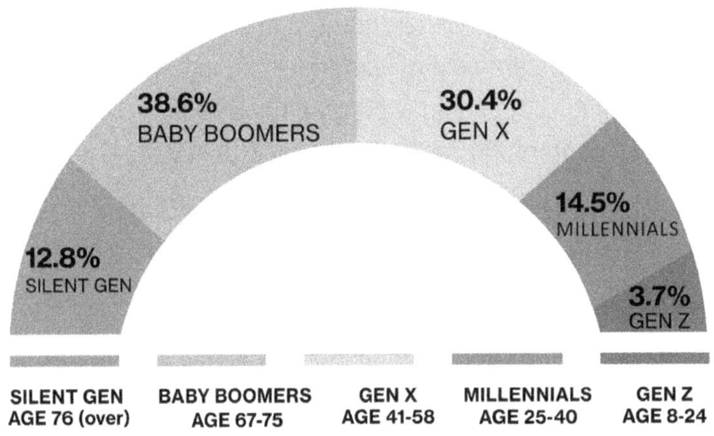

Generation Power Play in Present Times

[An Overview of the Dominant Generations]

- The Silent Generation: 12.8%
- The Baby Boomers: 38.6%
- Gen X: 30.4%
- The Millennials: 14.5%
- Gen Z: 3.7%

The above table makes it clear that **the generations that can be moulded or enhanced are Gen Z & more specifically Gen Alpha.**

The next logical question is; who will do that?

The responsibility majorly rests on the shoulders of the millennials with supporting roles from Gen X.

To nurture the smartness and responsibility inherent in Generation Alpha and Generation Z, parents and educators must embrace a new paradigm of learning – one rooted in coding and programming. Not coding & programming as in technology but coding & programming as in emotional & behavioural influence.

As the torchbearers of the future, it is imperative that these young minds are equipped with the tools to thrive in an increasingly complex world.

In the next chapter, we will understand in detail about these two important generations, The Millennials- who are the primary influencers in raising smart Star Kids and Gen Alpha, who will turn into these Smart Star Kids.

So, let's dive in without further ado

CHAPTER - 3

DECODING THE MILLENIALS & GEN ALPHA
Nurturing Smartness in Generation Alpha

Decoding The Millennials

Millennials, often heralded as the torchbearers of the digital revolution, bring with them a sense of self-confidence and ambition. Yet, they struggle with the realities of low-paying jobs, student debt, and the pervasive influence of technology on their lives.

➤ Alright, let's talk about millennials!

So, right now, they're the biggest group of people alive in the country, even more than the baby boomers. Armed with unprecedented access to information and technology, millennials navigate a landscape shaped by rapid globalization and rapid shifts in social norms.

And you know what? They've got some pretty cool stuff going on.

➤ First off, millennials are smart cookies.

Most of them have gone to college and got themselves some fancy degrees. They're also super confident in themselves, which is awesome. Plus, they're basically born with smartphones in their hands. They know all the latest tech tricks and are always on top of the newest gadgets.

Education lies at the heart of the millennial experience, with a significant portion of the generation attaining higher levels of education than the generation before them.

➤ But it's not all sunshine and rainbows for millennials.

They've got their fair share of problems too. One huge challenge they face is finding good jobs that pay well. Armed with degrees and vocational skills, they enter the workforce with high aspirations, only to be met with the harsh realities of low-paying jobs and unemployment. Lots of them end up stuck in low-paying jobs or even struggle to find work at all.

➢ **Oh, and let's not forget about college debt.**

Whew, that's a big one. Many millennials are swimming in student loans, trying to pay off those hefty bills. The ghost of college debt looms large, casting a shadow over their financial prospects and delaying major life milestones such as homeownership and starting a family.

➢ **Technology, while their core strength, also poses unique challenges**

While they are often tech-savvy, there's a growing concern about the pervasive nature of technology addiction within the generation. The constant flow of notifications and the charm of social media platforms present a double-edged sword, offering connectivity while simultaneously fuelling feelings of isolation and anxiety.

➢ **And then there's this thing called "cancel culture."**

Where people get called out on social media for saying or doing something that others don't like. Millennials have to deal with that a lot.

➢ **Plus, some of them have to juggle taking care of their aging parents.**

As they navigate the complexities of modern life, millennials also deal with the dual responsibilities of caring for aging parents while striving for personal and professional fulfillment.

The so-called sandwich generation, they find themselves stretched thin as they balance caregiving duties with their own aspirations and obligations.

> **And discrimination? Yeah, millennials face that too.**

Discrimination, whether based on race, gender, or sexual orientation, remains a sensitive issue for millennials, who champion diversity and inclusion as core values. Yet, despite their best efforts to shatter these prejudices, many still encounter prejudice and bias in various facets of life

> **But despite all these challenges, millennials are a resilient bunch.**

They continue to defy stereotypes and reshape societal norms, they're not afraid to speak up and fight for what they believe in. Millennials are leveraging their collective voice and digital savviness to champion causes ranging from environmental sustainability to mental health awareness. And with their smartness and tech-savviness, they're definitely making their mark on the world.

So, big applause to the millennials for being a generation that's not afraid to take on whatever comes their way!

As the torchbearers of the 21st century, they embody the spirit of resilience and innovation, forging a path forward in an ever-changing world.

Deciphering Gen Alpha

In contrast, Generation Alpha represents a paradigm shift in human evolution. Born entirely in the 21st century, they are the epitome of technological integration.

➤ **Let's talk about Generation Alpha, the youngsters who are kicking off their lives in the 21st century!**

These kids are something else, born into a world where technology is everywhere you look. Seriously, they've never known a time without smartphones, tablets, and all sorts of fancy gadgets.

➤ **Now, what sets Generation Alpha apart is their tech-savviness.**

I mean, these little ones seem to have been born with a natural knack for anything digital. They can swipe, tap, and click their way around devices like nobody's business. It's like they come out of the womb already knowing how to navigate the latest apps and games.

> **But it's not just about playing with gadgets.**

Generation Alpha is seriously smart. They seem to pick up on things way faster than previous generations. Complex ideas? No problem for these young minds. They're like sponges, soaking up knowledge and understanding concepts that might leave older folks scratching their heads.

And let's talk about their abilities. These kids can do some pretty impressive stuff for their age. From coding to creating content online, they're pushing boundaries and showing that age is just a number when it comes to what they can achieve.

> **Generation Alpha is growing up in a world where there are fewer kids around.**

That's because fertility rates are dropping in many places. But even with smaller numbers, these kiddos are making a big impact. And them being fewer helps focus attention and energy on them. They're shaping the future with their technological know-how and their boundless curiosity.

> **So, watch out world, because Generation Alpha is here!**

And they're ready to take on whatever challenges come their way, armed with their gadgets and their brains! And parents and a community who knows how to behaviourally code them into smart star kids.

From a young age, Alphas display an innate understanding of complex concepts and a proficiency in navigating the digital landscape. They are the architects of tomorrow, poised to redefine the boundaries of human potential.

As we delve into the coding of present-day children, we must understand the unique qualities of both Millennials and Generation Alpha which we have discussed above.

Millennials serve as the bridge between tradition and innovation, while Generation Alpha represents the frontline of technological progress.

In harnessing the potential of these generations, we embark on a journey towards a more prosperous and enlightened future.

By instilling the principles of behavioural coding and programming from an early age, we empower Generation Alpha and Generation Z to shape a world defined by innovation, creativity, and boundless possibility.

The generational code is not merely a blueprint for the future; it is a legacy of all that we as humans have learned, experienced and forged.

As we navigate the currents of change, let us embrace the transformative power of education and technology and mindful parenting, forging a path towards a brighter tomorrow for generations to come.

CHAPTER – 4

THE PRE-PREGNANCY CODE
The Key is in Beginning Right

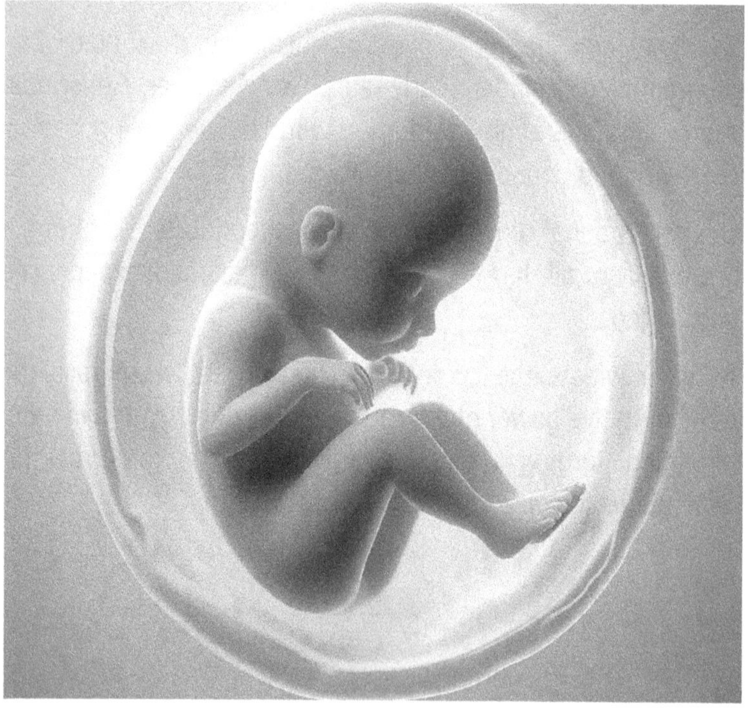

Clearing The Misconception About Pre-Conception

I'm sure you've all heard the age-old adage, "Like father, like son". Hold your horses before you start picturing images of a miniature version of yourself wreaking havoc around the house.

Things don't have to go the traditional way. With the right knowledge & wisdom you can choose and create the path, your children walk even before birth.

To show you how you can do this, we'll first need to address the elephant in the room:

How prepared are you to be a parent? What is the status of your education as a parent?

I have no pet educational theory, I believe only in the educational value of the parents' behaviour, both before and after the birth of their children.

That is why I never focus on sharing much about how to educate your children.

I focus on educating parents.

If parents do nothing to educate themselves, how can they expect to educate their children?

You see, there's a common misconception floating around that parenting is a skill you magically acquire the moment you cradle your bundle of joy in your arms. When people have children, everybody takes it for granted that they are capable of bringing them up. But this is often not the case: the parents, first and foremost, need to be educated and taught how to behave to be a beneficial influence on their children.

People who do not know the core of my programme criticize me initially: 'An educator? He's no educator; he never talks about the education of children.'

But as long as parents themselves are not up to the mark it makes no difference how many important educational theories you explain to them.

They bring children into the world and leave them to bring themselves up. The children do what they can on their own, and then, one day, they too have children in the same not-so-great conditions as their parents.

I am constantly astounded to see how many young men and women who want to get married never pause to think about preparing themselves for their future role as parents.

I'm sure at some time or the other, you've seen some young women who are pregnant, and you immediately thought, 'OMG, but she's a baby herself, and look at her, she's expecting a baby!'

What can you expect in such a scenario? It is far better not to have children if you are not properly prepared to do so; otherwise, I do assure you, it will cost you dearly.

If you're not prepped up and ready for the parenting game yourself, you might be setting yourself up for disappointment.

The Parental Prep Talk

Picture this, a couple of lovebirds, eyes gleaming with dreams of a perfect family completely unaware that there's a plot twist waiting for them!

Before you even consider diving into the realm of parenthood, have you stopped to ask yourself if you're truly prepared for the rollercoaster ride ahead?

You see, dear readers,

> **Bringing a child into this world isn't just about biology; it's about setting the stage for a star to be born and creating the right environment to nurture and develop them to their full potential of stardom.**

Yet, more often than not, we find ourselves witnessing scenes straight out of a comedy of errors rather than a heartwarming family drama.

Choosing Your Co-Stars in The Drama of Life

But what if I told you that you can write your own script? — You're the casting director of your own family blockbuster.

But here's perhaps the most powerful secret of life that most of us are blissfully unaware of. That you possess the divine power to attract little bundles of genius into your fold, consciously.

Bringing a child into this world is not meant to be a random act just because it is the done thing or the accidental outcome of a night of passion.

It is something that you can do mindfully for amazing results. Yet instead of doing this with grace and intention, some of us are stumbling through the process in a haze of intoxication and impulsiveness.

Children are not born into a particular family by chance.

Whether you realize it or not — and most of the time you are very far from realizing it — **it is the parents who cause those particular beings to incarnate as their children.**

In this light, you should consciously endeavour to attract divine beings, creatures of genius, into their family.

You have the tremendous power of choosing your children — and you are unaware of it.

And with great power comes great responsibility, therefore as parents, it is your responsibility to prepare yourself, even before you conceive.

So the whole question needs to be re-examined from the beginning, and the beginning is the conception of a child.

Sadly, it never occurs to parents that they should prepare themselves for months, even years, before performing this sacred act.

Regrettably, as often as not, children are conceived after their parents have been out on a spree, eating and drinking too much. This is the occasion most parents choose – if one can even refer to it as 'choosing' in these conditions!

Why don't you rather choose a moment of peace and lucidity, a moment of deep connection and true harmony to make love and bring a child into this world?

But, no. Most of you pick a moment when you are besotted by alcohol and not fully conscious of what you are doing.

If this is the subconscious condition of many parents at the moment of conceiving a child! Imagine, what elements they introduce into a child conceived under these chaotic conditions.

> **A child that comes into the world burdened with such elements of chaos, randomness and accidental conception is the first victim of its own parents.**

I ask you now, who do you think most needs to be educated?

Yes, now you are getting it right— The parents, of course!

If parents lie and cheat other people in the presence of their children, how can they possibly hope to educate them & inculcate in them the principles of honesty and integrity?

The Ripple Effect of Parental Discord

Now, brace yourselves for a reality check, folks. Your actions, and your vibes, all send ripples through the very fabric of your family dynamics.

It has already been ascertained that a baby can fall ill and show signs of nervous disorders when its parents quarrel. Even if it is not in the same room at the time, a quarrel creates a discordant atmosphere which the baby immediately picks up, for it is still very connected to its parents.

The baby is not consciously aware of the disharmony but this does not prevent it from being extremely receptive, and its etheric body feels the shock. That baby might not understand the words being thrown around like daggers, but their little etheric antennas are picking up on the discord faster than you can say "toddler tantrum."

Love vs. Animal Instincts

Let's address love. perhaps the most misused word in our language. No, not the fleeting, superficial kind of love that flickers and fades like a candle in the wind. I'm talking about the kind of love that prompts you to take a long, hard look in the mirror and ask yourself, "Am I really showing up for my child?"

Parents must be more conscious of their responsibilities. Sometimes I see parents behaving so unbelievably stupidly that I ask them, 'Tell me... do you even love your child?'

Of course, they get very indignant, and say, 'What? Love him/her? Of course, we love them!' But I feel obliged to tell them, 'I don't believe it. If you loved your child, you'd change your attitude and start trying to correct some of the things that have such a disastrous effect on them.

Because, my dear friends, if all you're interested in is the pursuit of pleasure, then brace yourselves for a rude awakening.

Parenting isn't just about indulging in momentary gratification; it's about laying the groundwork for a future brimming with love, growth, and infinite possibilities.

Most people are content to live like animals: they eat,

drink and procreate like animals. There is no spiritual content to what they do.

Love simply doesn't come into it. All they're interested in is pleasure, and for a few moments of pleasure they are going to have to pay – and their children are going to have to pay – for the rest of their lives!

Tell me again, do you really want me to concern myself with your children?

Definitely Not!

It is you who are my first concern and indirectly, through you, I am already doing something for the children you have now and for those you will have in the future.

But guess what?

It Starts with You —

So, dear readers, before you embark on the exhilarating journey of parenthood, take a moment to reflect on your own readiness. Are you equipped with the tools, the mindset, and the love necessary to raise the next generation of trailblazers?

CHAPTER – 5

CODE PREGNANCY
Navigating the Maze of Brain Development

Brain It Up

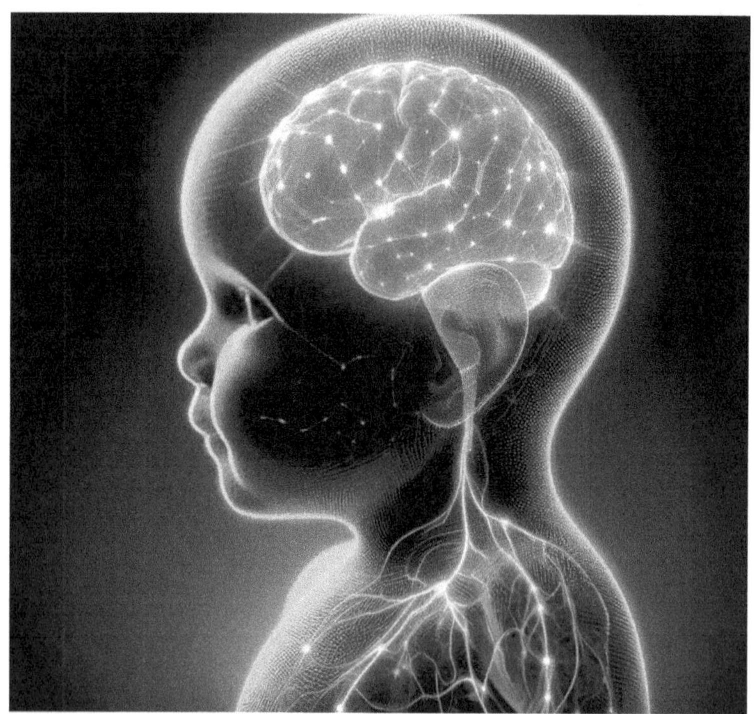

Embarking on the journey of pregnancy is like strapping into a rollercoaster ride of development, especially when it comes to brain growth.

As parents, you will need to buckle up, because from the get-go, at just six weeks, the embryo's brain and nervous system kickstart their journey of complex development.

Would you believe that this development that starts at the embryonic stage continues for a pretty long time and doesn't wrap up until around the age of 25?

Allow me to give you the picture— Though the brainstem is the first part of the brain to take the lead in development, calling the shots on essential functions, other higher parts aren't just sitting around twiddling their thumbs, they are evolving simultaneously but at their own leisurely pace.

The cerebral cortex– the part of the brain that controls thought, feeling, language and the senses, is like the grand conductor of the entire brain development orchestra– It is the last to mature and begins functioning shortly before a baby is born.

It's like a symphony orchestra where every section tunes up at its own tempo.

But here's the kicker: your emotional state decides the path your baby's brain development takes. It's simple, your vibe sets the mood for the party.

Your Vibe is The Key

When you feel happy and calm, it allows your baby to develop in a happy, calm environment. Keep the vibes happy and zen, and you set the stage for a serene little nest of development.

But toss in stress and anxiety, and you might stir up a hormonal mosh pit that affects your baby's growth, potentially leading to an early arrival or a featherweight champ at birth.

Emotions like stress and anxiety can increase particular hormones in your body, which can affect your baby's developing body and brain. During pregnancy, stress can increase the chances of having a premature baby (born before 37 weeks of pregnancy) or a low-birthweight baby (weighing less than 2 kg).

Now, the intention of sharing this information is not to worry or pressurize you but to empower & prepare you.

There is a chance that you might now be worried about oh, how am I going to be stress-free

Don't worry, I am also sharing with you the tools to remain stress-free.

Yoga & Meditation To The Rescue

Enter yoga & meditation into the scenario. Doctors also recommend these to keep both mom and baby in tip-top shape. It's like the soothing soundtrack to your baby's brain-building montage. Yoga & meditation have been shown to keep anxiety, depression & panic away. They foster a state of calm & peace.

➤ Yoga combines intentional flexibility & movement with structured breathing, this helps in keeping depression away. Breathing in a slow, rhythmic pattern activates the nervous system and limits & blocks the release of cortisol, which can lead to depression.

➤ The stretching & breathing involved in yoga help improve blood flow to your heart. This better blood flow as a result means more oxygen-rich blood going to your baby. This ensures that your baby's brain & body development stays on track.

➤ Meditation helps you balance your emotions and stay calm during the pregnancy which helps in a smooth and stress-free pregnancy. It also helps you stay calm during your labour ensuring there is no trauma to the foetus either during pregnancy or delivery.

The Mother is Indeed The Motherboard in This Program

And here's a fascinating twist: just like planting a seed in the soil, the seed a man plants in a woman carries its own genetic punch. It's like a pre-programmed recipe for your little one's talents and quirks. However, once the seed is fertilized in the womb, during the nine months of pregnancy, the mother becomes the ultimate supplier, feeding into this genetic blueprint, and adding her brushstrokes to the canvas of creation.

The mother is complete in herself, having all the resources needed and supplying them to the foetus to carry out the program to completion.

Therefore it is essential that the mother is kept in the best of health physically with the appropriate diet & exercise as well as in emotional & mental health by providing a stress-free and supportive environment.

Protecting the Energy & Aura of The Foetus

While most people take care of the physical, mental & emotional health of pregnant women, they ignore a very crucial aspect of health— spiritual & energetic health.

Yes, there is more to this baby saga than meets the eye!

Ever noticed how pregnant women suddenly channel their inner divas and are often subject to all kinds of whims and uncontrolled impulses they normally would never have? Certain weird cravings or desires are pretty common.

But what people do not know is why this happens.

Here is the reason that is not commonly known or believed.

So powerful yet vulnerable is the Aura [Energy Body] of a pregnant woman carrying a divine new life that she often ends up attracting astral entities who look forward to using her child as a body to live in.

Wanting control over the foetus, they try to influence the mother and interfere with the excellent gold-plating she is doing on the foetus by providing the right resources and environment in the womb. They know that if this is not done properly they will be able to go in and out of the child and feed on it. When this happens, it is plainly visible in the child's behaviour quite early on in life. They will show symptoms of disharmony such as anger, withdrawal, destruction etc.

They might be playing host to some dubious entities vying for a backstage pass to influence the munchkin. Sneaky, huh?

Therefore it is essential to learn to protect the energy of the mother by keeping her in harmonious environments and ensuring that she stays in high vibrational energy.

> Ensure that you only interact with high-vibrational people and avoid toxic people.

> Whenever you leave home, first build an imaginary bubble of protection around you and set the intention that only positive energy will touch you.

➢ Once you come home or after any interaction with others. Actively cleanse your energy by having a bath if possible or by at least washing your feet.

➢ Sage, incense and clean your home regularly.

So, there you have it, folks. Pregnancy isn't just about baby bumps and cravings—it's a pretty wild ride of brainy proportions, with a dash of cosmic drama thrown in for good measure. So buckle up, prepare and get ready to enjoy the journey!

☐ ☐ ☐ ☐

CHAPTER - 6

AND THE BABY IS HERE...
Nurturing with Love and Education

Mindful Nursing

You as a couple and as expecting parents have consistently done all the work to ensure you are ready to be woke & Conscious parents. You have taken care to conceive and carry your baby harmoniously, lovingly, joyfully and keeping the energy of both the mother and the foetus protected.

Everything that could be seeded & coded before and during

pregnancy has been done and finally, the D day is here.

Your baby, your bundle of joy is actually in your arms.

Surrounding the baby with love and joy, and whispering positive affirmations into its ears is essential, but most important is how you as a mother nurse the infant.

When a woman nurses her baby, she must do so with conscious attention, totally focused on the child, fully present in the moment and talking to it.

This practice of 'mindful nursing' infuses the act of nourishment with something more profound—her heart and soul, her very essence. An infant nourished in this loving manner will cherish its mother for eternity. Even if the mother is neither highly educated nor conventionally beautiful, her child will adore her.A child nourished in this manner will form a deep bond with the mother and will feel safe & secure.

This feeling of safety and security fostered as an infant carries forth in childhood, adolescence and adulthood. Such babies grow up to be people with high self-esteem & low insecurities and because they are secure and feel worthy themselves, as a result, they find it easy to see the good in others as well. Such people are confident, trust their own decisions and do not self-doubt.

A child must be conceived in love and then nourished with love.

However, with the changing norms and stressful lifestyles today, it is challenging for mothers to be conscious and mindful. More often than not, the consciousness of most mothers today remains narrow and personal.

Many have not yet comprehended the profound importance of their role as educators. True education, which should ideally begin from birth, often goes undelivered as parents are not aware of it and no schools or colleges teach this.

This lack of conscious and mindful education right since birth is leading to a decline in overall societal values. To counteract this trend, it is vital for parents and caregivers as well as educators to understand the stages of child brain development and the role of nurturing at each phase.

Let's discuss and understand these better below.

Brain Development Timeline

Sensory Motor Stage (Birth to 2 Years)

During the sensory, motor stage, children learn about the world using their senses. It is a period of rapid development where infants begin to understand their environment through touch, sight, sound, and movement. Activities like pointing at objects and naming them, engaging in back-and-forth conversation, and playing interactive games are crucial. These activities not only enhance their sensory experiences but also foster early cognitive and linguistic skills.

Preoperational Stage (Ages 2 to 7)

In the preoperational stage, cognitive growth continues at a fast pace. Children begin to develop memory and imagination. They start to understand symbols and language more deeply. This is a critical time to encourage their curiosity by answering their questions, helping them

---

turn the pages of books, and engaging them in discussions about what they read and see. These interactions lay the foundation for their future learning and social skills.

Concrete Operational Stage (Ages 7 to 11)

During the concrete operational stage, children gain a better understanding of logical operations and can handle more complex ideas. They start to think logically about concrete events but still struggle with abstract concepts. This stage is marked by the development of organized and rational thinking, which is essential for academic success and problem-solving in everyday life.

So here's a step-by-step blueprint for how you can code the right traits and characteristics into your child through the simple age-old tool of reading.

Step-by-Step Guide: Reading and Coding Development

Newborn to 1 Year
+ Point at objects and name them (e.g., dog, cat)
+ Talk back and forth with the baby
+ Engage in playful reading to develop recognition skills

1 Year to 2 Years
+ Answer questions with a smile
+ Encourage pointing and naming of objects
+ Involve the child in turning pages to enhance motor skills

2 Years to 3 Years
+ Ask questions about the book's content
+ Discuss pictures and meanings of words
+ Let the child choose books to foster a love for reading

3 Years to 4 Years
+ Point out letters and numbers
+ Create stories together from the pictures
+ Discuss characters and their roles to build comprehension

4 Years to 5 Years
+ Have the child narrate the story
+ Encourage writing and drawing related to the book
+ Discuss the meaning of the story and words for deeper understanding

Reading and Coding: A Step-by-Step Guide

Newborn to 1 Year : At this stage, point at things and name them (e.g., dog, cat, house). Talk back and forth with your baby. Engage in playful activities while reading to them. These interactions help in developing their auditory and visual recognition skills.

1 Year to 2 Years : Smile and answer your child's questions. Encourage them to point at objects and name them. Involve them in the reading process by having them help turn the pages. This promotes their motor skills and reinforces their understanding of language and objects.

2 Years to 3 Years : Ask them questions about the book. Discuss the pictures and what the words mean. Let them choose the book they want to read. Setting goals and rewarding their reading efforts can motivate them to engage more deeply with books, fostering a love for reading.

3 Years to 4 Years : Point out letters and numbers. Look at pictures together and create stories about them. Discuss different characters and their roles. Encourage your child to express their thoughts about the story. These activities enhance their comprehension and critical thinking skills.

4 Years to 5 Years : Have your child narrate the story. Encourage them to write and draw. Discuss the meaning of the story and the words used. Engage in conversations about the content, asking them to share their interpretations. This helps in developing their narrative skills and understanding of complex concepts.

By following these guidelines, parents can ensure their children receive a rich and nurturing educational experience from the earliest stages of life.

The emphasis on love, attention, and interactive learning lays a strong foundation for their emotional and intellectual development, preparing them for future challenges and opportunities.

Children who are given ample attention to and are read to develop a curious, learning-orienteand mindset, and their cognitive and problem-solving skills are also better.

They approach life with an open, growth-oriented mindset. Plus the bonding with their caregivers while reading inculcates in them a sense of community which helps them be better team players later in life and at work. Reading also helps fire the imagination leading to out-of-the-box lateral thinking

In summary, the role of a mother—or any primary caregiver—extends far beyond the basic act of feeding. It encompasses a profound responsibility to nurture the child's mind and spirit with love, attention, and education.

By recognizing and embracing this role, parents can profoundly impact their child's life, fostering a bond of love and admiration that lasts a lifetime and setting the stage for a brighter, more educated and compassionate future.

CHAPTER - 7

CODE OF CONDUCT
The Power of Words and Actions

The Magic of a Mother's Whisper

Visualize this—In a serene, dim-lit nursery, a mother sits quietly by the cot of her sleeping baby. She gently picks up the infant and holds it close, her heart overflowing with love and hope for the future. As she softly strokes the baby's head, she begins to murmur, "My baby, I love you very much. I want you to be full of radiant light, divine life, intelligence, strength, purity and loving-kindness..."

This practice, although it might seem unusual or even nonsensical to some, is grounded in the profound understanding that words carry immense power.

I am sure all of you have heard of wishes & boons being granted by powerful saints and wise/holy men & women, spells being cast by powerful people or even curses being given by angered saints not only in stories but in real life too. How do you think these come true? Simple— it's all the power of words. Words have the power to affect your subconscious mind and thus your actions & decisions.

Parents must learn to use the power of words to do only good to their children, and I have already given you a method for this in the opening paragraph of this chapter.

The mother's words, whispered with love and intention, are believed to penetrate the baby's subconscious mind, laying the foundation for the virtues and strengths she envisions for her child. Despite the baby's lack of conscious understanding, these positive affirmations are recorded deep within its being, shaping its future in subtle but significant ways.

Mothers are encouraged to engage in this heartfelt dialogue with their babies daily, both morning and evening. A mother should do this every day and every evening. She should talk softly to her baby, gently stroking its head, telling it of the strength and all the virtues and qualities it already possesses and which it will learn to develop later on. She should talk to her baby about its future, about how happy it is going to be and how it will become a noble, exceptional being.

By consistently expressing their desires for their child's happiness, strength, and nobility and any other positive characteristics they wish to code, mothers can imbue their little ones with a sense of security and positivity that will guide them throughout their lives.

The simple act of whispering poetic, positive and wonderful words can become a powerful tool in nurturing a child's inner world, filling it with light and love.

Leading by Example: The Best Education

As children grow, their learning is not limited to what they hear but is significantly influenced by what they observe.

Parents often wait until their children reach a certain level of intellectual understanding before beginning formal education, relying heavily on explanations.

However, real education transcends mere words and explanations; it is rooted in the power of example.

Imagine a young child watching their parent meticulously washing and cleaning dishes, organizing the house, or preparing a meal. Without a single word of instruction, the child observes, absorbs, and imitates these actions.

This is because children are like little monkeys; they learn by copying what they see. **By demonstrating positive behaviors and skills in daily life, parents provide a living example for their children to follow.**

Show them how to take care of their belongings, how to be organized, and how to contribute to household chores. This hands-on learning approach fosters a sense of responsibility and independence in children, enabling them to develop essential life skills naturally and effortlessly.

Building Resilience: Strength Through Challenges

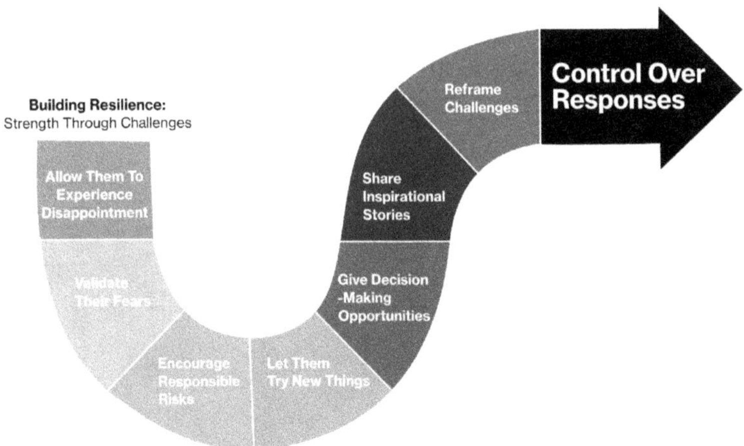

Resilience, the ability to bounce back from adversity, is a crucial trait that can be cultivated from a young age.

Here are eight practical strategies that provide a complete roadmap to help build resilience in children:

1. Allow Them To Experience Disappointment

Don't try to overprotect your child or lay out everything to perfection for them. Also if they fail or do not get what they want, let them take responsibility for their part in it, do not encourage them to put the entire blame on to others. Allow children to experience disappointment. It teaches them that sadness is a natural part of life and that it doesn't last forever. This understanding helps them develop emotional endurance and balance.

2. Validate Their Fears

Acknowledge and validate their fears, for them they are real. Do not just brush aside these fears or tell them not to be silly or sissy, asking them to just get over them. Instead, help them create plans to face and overcome these fears, providing a sense of empowerment and control.

3. Encourage Responsible Risks

Encourage children to take responsible risks and experience the natural consequences of their actions. This fosters learning and growth from real-life experiences. Helps them feel empowered and makes them more confident.

4. Let Them Try New Things

Motivate them to try new activities, make mistakes, and learn from those mistakes. This promotes a growth mindset and resilience in the face of failure. Exploring new avenues ignites their thinking and imagination, encouraging them to think out of the box, leading to invention & innovation.

5. Give Decision-Making Opportunities

Give them opportunities to make their own decisions. Support them in problem-solving, which builds confidence and critical thinking skills. Begin small, let them decide what they want to eat or wear, which book they want to read at bedtime, what activity they want to do on the weekend etc.

6. Share Inspirational Stories

Share with them stories of people who have faced hardships and emerged stronger. People who are role models can influence their thinking and choices. These narratives can inspire and provide valuable lessons on resilience and perseverance. This models not only inspiration but also possibility for them. It makes them believe that they too can achieve what they want. It encourages them to aim higher and teaches them to value and cultivate positive traits.

7. Reframe Challenges

Don't exhibit a panicked or defeatist attitude towards challenges. Instead, present challenges as temporary problems and opportunities for learning rather than insurmountable obstacles. This perspective helps children develop a positive and proactive approach to difficulties. Also, teach them that challenges are an inevitable part of life.

8. Control Over Responses

Teach children that while they cannot control everything that happens to them, they can control how they respond. This empowers them to manage their reactions and emotions effectively. Emotional intelligence can be fostered right from childhood by responding rather than reacting to situations.

Exploring the Natural World:
Fostering Environmental Awareness

In addition to emotional and intellectual development, fostering a connection with the natural world is essential. Take your child on journeys of learning and adventure, exploring the beauty and diversity of nature. Teach them about the importance of every natural component, from plants to ecosystems, and explain how global warming affects our planet.

Make these learning experiences entertaining and fun!

For example, turn a walk in the park into a mini-adventure, discovering different types of plants and discussing their roles in the environment. This not only educates but also instills a sense of wonder and appreciation for the natural world.

The Role of Genetics and Environment in Intelligence

Intelligence is influenced by a combination of genetic and environmental factors. While children may be born with the potential to be gifted, the environment in which they are raised plays a crucial role in developing their innate abilities.

Research suggests that environmental influences can significantly impact measured intelligence, potentially adding 20-40 IQ points.

Parents who provide a nurturing and stimulating environment can enhance their children's intellectual & emotional development. This includes ensuring good nutrition, safe housing, engaging educational experiences and deep emotional connections. By doing so, they help unlock their children's potential, allowing them to thrive and excel.

Raising resilient, intelligent, emotionally balanced and environmentally aware children requires a multifaceted approach.

Through the power of loving words, leading by example, fostering resilience, and creating enriching experiences, parents can profoundly influence their children's development. The journey of parenthood is filled with opportunities to shape young minds and hearts, guiding them toward a future of happiness, strength, and nobility.

By embracing these methods, parents can provide their children with the tools they need to navigate life with confidence and grace.

□ □ □ □

CHAPTER - 8

Decoding The Evolving Adolescent Brain
Cultivating Resilience and Empathy in Generation Z

The Brain's Amazing Journey: From Chaos to Connection

As children transition into their teenage years, their brains undergo remarkable changes. The brain, much like a bustling city, continues to build and strengthen its interconnected networks of neurons. These intricate neural pathways are essential for forming memories and linking new information with previous learning. It's a dynamic process that significantly influences both academic growth and social development.

As the brain matures, more and more fibers grow and the brain becomes increasingly interconnected. These interconnected networks of neurons are very important to the formation of memories and the connection of new learning to previous learning. As neural networks form, the child learns both academically and socially.

It's also the period where hormones are raging & teenagers are rebelling and parents are pulling out their hair in frustration. However, it doesnt have to be so, and that is exactly what I will show you in this chapter.

Understanding the science behind adolescent behavior, particularly tantrums, offers a window into their emotional world. Teenagers, despite their growing cognitive abilities, often experience intense emotions and stresses that they struggle to regulate.

Their brains, still maturing, aren't fully equipped to manage these emotions logically. **This developmental stage explains why teens might resort to crying, whining, or acting out— they're communicating their stress in the only way they know how.**

The Disconnect: Bridging the Generational Gap

One of the pressing issues today is the breakdown in relationships between parents and their teenage children. Many parents find themselves unable to connect with their children on a deep, emotional level.

The vibrational energy of love, wisdom, and strength that should ideally flow from parent to child often gets lost in the hustle and bustle of daily life.

One of the main reasons why relations between parents and children break down so frequently these days is that parents have become incapable of influencing their children through their own vibrations. They have become incapable of impregnating them with their love, wisdom, strength and life.

The purpose of my work is to show parents how to work on their children with intelligence and consciousness.

Imagine the power of a mother's love, not just as a fleeting feeling when her child is sick or seeking affection, but as a constant, empowering force. This enduring love, imbued with wisdom and strength, can create a profound impact on a child's development. However, many parents struggle to maintain this connection, as other feelings and distractions quickly take precedence.

Planting Seeds in the Subconscious:
The Power of Early Experiences

Even if adolescents don't fully grasp the lessons and values their parents impart, these seeds are planted deep within their subconscious minds.

Over time, these lessons resurface, guiding their decisions and actions. Teenagers attending talks or witnessing significant events might not understand everything at the moment, but these experiences are recorded in their subconscious, waiting to influence their conscious lives later on.

So don't give up on your teenagers, keep communicating with them positively & keep loving them, they may not respond how you expect them to, but it's all being recorded in their subconscious and it's shaping their subconscious mind and will affect their decisions later in life.

Take, for instance, the simple practice of bringing children to watch the sunrise. Some might argue that teens should stay in bed, but these moments are invaluable. Witnessing the beauty and tranquility of a sunrise can instill a sense of awe and appreciation for nature, subtly shaping their worldview and resilience.

Building Resilience: Preparing for Life's Challenges

Parents who aspire for their children to assume important responsibilities in the future must prepare them to face life's difficulties right from the beginning. **Shielding teens from every hardship does them a disservice.** Instead, they should be exposed to challenges that build their resilience and empathy.

Consider those who grow up in challenging environments and rise through their own hard work. They develop a deep understanding and compassion for others who struggle because they know what it feels like to suffer. This empathy and resilience are crucial traits for future leaders, enabling them to connect with and support those they lead.

As in the previous chapter, here too, I am sharing with you an 8-step road map to coding & guiding teenagers to becoming extraordinary human beings.

Strategies for Cultivating Resilience and Empathy

1. Foster Emotional Intelligence

Teach teenagers about their emotions and how to manage them. Encourage open conversations about feelings and stress, helping them develop the vocabulary to express themselves better.

2. Model Resilient Behavior

Demonstrate resilience in your own life. Show your children how you handle setbacks and stress with grace and perseverance. Your actions will speak louder than any words.

3. Encourage Responsible Independence

Allow teens to take on responsibilities and make decisions, even if it means they might fail. These experiences teach valuable lessons in accountability and problem-solving.

4. Expose Them to Diverse Experiences

Broaden their horizons by exposing them to different environments and challenges. Whether it's volunteering, traveling, or engaging in new activities, these experiences build character and empathy.

5. Practice Positive Reinforcement

Acknowledge and celebrate their efforts and successes. Positive reinforcement encourages them to continue striving and builds their self-confidence.

6. Teach the Value of Hard Work

Instill a strong work ethic by involving them in household chores, part-time jobs, or community service. Understanding the value of hard work fosters resilience and a sense of accomplishment.

7. Nurture Compassionate Leadership

Encourage them to take on leadership roles in school or community projects. Leadership experiences help them understand the importance of empathy and support in guiding others.

8. Cultivate a Growth Mindset

Promote the belief that abilities and intelligence can be developed through dedication and hard work. This mindset helps them view challenges as opportunities for growth rather than obstacles.

The Path to Empowerment

Raising resilient, empathetic, and intelligent teenagers requires a balanced approach that combines love, understanding, and practical experience. By understanding the unique developmental stage of the adolescent brain, parents can better empathize with their children and guide them through their emotional and social challenges.

Empowering teenagers involves more than just protecting them from hardships; it requires preparing them to face life's challenges head-on. Through consistent love, positive reinforcement, and exposure to diverse experiences, parents can help their teens develop the resilience and empathy needed to succeed in life.

In the journey of parenting, every moment, every whisper of encouragement, and every challenge faced together contributes to the growth of a well-rounded, compassionate, and capable individual.

The seeds planted today will blossom into the leaders and changemakers of tomorrow, ready to navigate the complexities of life with strength and grace.

CHAPTER - 9

The Essence of True Education
Igniting The Light in Gen Z

The Illusion of Material Progress

In recent years, substantial efforts have been made to enhance the educational experiences of children and adolescents. The improvements in schools are evident: they boast larger, better-equipped buildings with modern laboratories, radio, cinema, television, sports grounds, swimming pools, and more. These advancements are indeed praiseworthy and contribute significantly to the material side of education. However, a critical question remains: are the children themselves any better for it?

I am often asked for advice about how to educate children, and I reply, 'As you know, a great deal has been done in recent years concerning children and adolescents, but if you look at the improvements in the schools and so on, you will see that they all concern the external, material side. The schools are bigger and better. Yes, but what about the children? Are they any better? I'm afraid not!

Sadly, the answer often appears to be no.

The focus on external improvements has overshadowed the inner development of young minds.

The assumption that better books and advanced learning aids are all children need has not yielded the miraculous results that many anticipated.

Despite these advancements, the character and behavior of the youth have not significantly improved. This realization has led many to question the effectiveness of current educational methods.

The Power of Example

The heart of the problem lies in the absence of living examples. Teachers, lecturers, and parents often overlook the profound impact their own behavior has on children. Young people possess an uncanny ability to discern truth and authenticity, much like animals who rely on instinct. Their judgment is often unerring, making it all the more crucial for those in positions of influence to lead by example.

The opinion of children holds immense importance because of their innate sense of truth. While the judgment of an adult may not cause much concern, the judgment of a child can be terrifying in its accuracy. This instinctual ability underscores the necessity for educators and parents to embody the virtues they wish to instill in their children.

The Inner Light of Parents and Educators

Parents must not fall into the illusion that providing material instruction satisfies the essential needs of their children. This misconception can lead to a disconnect between generations, an illusion which can only lead to war between the generations.

Children, armed with new knowledge and a sense of superiority from their education, often clash with their parents, leading to tension and disappointment— the parents are unhappy and disappointed to see that their children are ungrateful, rude and violent.

However, they have only themselves to blame!

The root of this issue lies in the parents' failure to cultivate an inner light and strength that commands respect and admiration. Why have they never done anything to acquire the inner light and strength that will always impress their children with their wisdom? This should be the goal of all parents: to become so noble and high-minded, so radiant and strong that they will be exemplary.

The goal of every parent should be to become noble, high-minded, radiant, and strong, setting an exemplary standard for their children. Before attempting to educate others, one must first educate themselves. Just as a population mirrors its leader, so too do children mirror their parents. A parent who exudes kindness, nobility, and integrity will inspire similar qualities in their children.

The Exalted Nature of Teaching

If teachers and professors are worn out at the end of the school year, it is not because it is so exhausting to take care of children but because all too often they work with a mercenary mentality: their main concern is to earn their living. They are not interested in the children.

They simply try to get through their work as quickly as possible, never stopping to reflect on the exalted nature of their calling, which is to look after the souls of all these children that heaven has entrusted to their care.

It goes without saying that children have failings, but once you embark upon a career as an educator you assume the obligation to think of the children's future, to be attentive and considerate towards them, in fact, to love them.

And as all children are responsive to affection and kindness, after a time they will begin to respond and to change. Teaching is not merely a profession; it is a calling of the highest order. Educators are entrusted with the souls of the children they teach, and this responsibility should never be taken lightly. Unfortunately, many teachers and professors approach their work with a mercenary mentality, viewing it primarily as a means to earn a living. This lack of genuine interest in the children leads to burnout and dissatisfaction.

True educators recognize the exalted nature of their role. They understand that children, despite their failings, are highly responsive to affection and kindness. By thinking of the children's future, being attentive and considerate, and genuinely loving them, educators can foster an environment where children feel valued and understood. Over time, this approach will encourage positive changes in behavior and attitude.

Nourishing the Mind

Now, everyone is at liberty to do what they please. However, I can predict in advance what the results will be, depending on whether you nourish your mind with life or spend all your time immersed in books.

So far, if you have not grasped the difference between nourishing your mind and merely reading, please understand it now.

Even if you never read books; read the book of nature, read people, their faces and their hearts. Above all, read the sun; the sun is my daily reading. Every day it reveals something new to me, and here in this book also, I have passed its revelations on to you.

Once you begin to learn from Mother Nature, in time, you too will begin to read fewer books, because you will have learned to read the book of living nature.

The distinction between nourishing the mind and merely reading books is crucial. While books provide valuable knowledge, they are not the sole source of wisdom. True nourishment of the mind comes from engaging with the world around us, observing nature, and understanding the human heart.

For instance, the sun, a symbol of constancy and renewal, offers daily lessons to those who take the time to observe it. Every day, the sun reveals something new, providing insights that can be shared and applied in life. This approach to learning—reading the book of living nature—encourages a deeper connection with the world and a more profound understanding of oneself and others.

The Path Forward

In conclusion, the path to effective education lies not in the continual enhancement of material conditions but in the cultivation of inner virtues.

Parents and educators must strive to become living examples of the values they wish to impart. By doing so, they will not only improve their own lives but also profoundly influence the character and behavior of the younger generation.

This inner radiance and strength, manifesting externally, will create a nurturing environment where children can truly thrive and grow into compassionate, respectful, and enlightened individuals

Youth who are trained in this manner will turn out to be truly special and impact the world around them positively and magnificently.

□ □ □ □

9 789363 385252